PRAYERS FROM THE *IMITATION OF CHRIST*

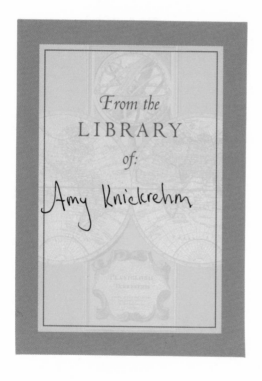

From the
LIBRARY
of:

Amy Knickrehm

PRAYERS FROM THE *IMITATION OF CHRIST*

Thomas à Kempis

Edited by Ronald Klug

MINNEAPOLIS

PRAYERS FROM THE *IMITATION OF CHRIST*

Cover design by David Meyer
Text design by James Satter

Library of Congress Cataloging-in-Publication Data

Imitatio Christi. English. Selections.
    Prayers from the Imitation of Christ / Thomas à Kempis : edited by Ronald Klug.
      p.   cm.
    Includes bibliographical references and index.
    ISBN 0-8066-2989-4 (alk. paper)
    1. Prayers. I. Thomas, à Kempis, 1380-1471. II. Klug, Ron.
III. Title.
BV245.I495 1996
242'.8—dc20
                                96-29161
                                CIP

The paper used in this publication meets the minimum requirements of American National Standard for Information Sciences—Permanence of Paper for Printed Library Materials, ANSI Z329.48-1984.   ∞

Manufactured in the U.S.A.   AF 9-2989

00 99 98 97 96   1 2 3 4 5 6 7 8 9 10

For Theodore Hartwig,
who introduced me to the
Imitation of Christ

CONTENTS

INTRODUCTION

For more than five centuries, Christians of all denominations have found guidance and strength and comfort in the devotional classic the *Imitation of Christ*. Some have said it is the most widely read Christian book after the Bible. Among those who have acknowledged their debt to the *Imitation* are Thomas More, Ignatius Loyola, John Wesley, Dr. Samuel Johnson, and Dag Hammarskjöld. Matthew Arnold called the book, "The most exquisite document, after those of the New Testament, of all that the Christian spirit has ever inspired."

The *Imitation of Christ* was written by Thomas à Kempis (c. 1380–1471), a German native who had moved to Deventer, Netherlands, around 1392 and became a member of the Brethren of the Common Life, a group of clergy and lay people whose purpose was to deepen the religious life of the time, promote sound learning, and care for the poor. Thomas joined the Congregation of Windesheim at the Agnietenberg monastery, took his vows in 1408, was ordained in 1413, and devoted his life to copying manuscripts and directing novices.

Thomas wrote his widely renowned devotional book *Imitatio Christi* in 1427 to encourage people to follow the teachings of Christ and to imitate Christ's life. At first, handwritten copies were made and circulated, until 1472, when it was set in type for the first time. It quickly spread across Europe, and 1,800 editions and translations were in circulation by 1779.

The *Imitation of Christ* is divided into four books. Book I contains general counsel on the Christian life. Books II

9

and III give further advice on the inner life of devotion.
Book IV deals with the Sacrament of Holy Communion.

Scattered throughout the four books, but especially
in Book III, are prayers of great dignity and simple
strength—prayers of confession, praise, longing for God,
and love of God. These prayers still speak for us today
because they deal with the basic relationship of the soul
with God. They can help us put into words our deepest
longing for God and for God's help.

I have gathered these prayers from the *Imitation* and para-
phrased them into the language of today. In some cases I
have divided very long prayers into several shorter ones, and
I have condensed some prayers by eliminating repetitions.
I have tried always to remain faithful to the original spirit
and meaning.

Several things strike me about these prayers:

1. They are profoundly biblical. One often hears echoes of the
words of Jesus, of the Psalms, and of the prophets. Someone
has counted 850 scripture passages that are quoted or
alluded to in the *Imitation.*

2. The prayers are God-centered. Their dominant note is ado-
ration. They magnify God, praising God's greatness over
against our littleness, and God's goodness over against our
sin. They emphasize the majesty of God far above all created
things. The *Imitation* has been criticized for taking too low a
view of creation. This may be true, yet I wonder if today,
when there is so much emphasis on self and on material
things, this is not a voice calling us back to sanity. Perhaps
this emphasis on the transcendence of God is a corrective to

our frenzied search for self-fulfillment, luxuries, and pleasures. Over against all that, the *Imitation* cries, "God *alone*, above all things."

3. *The prayers express our total dependence on God.* They echo the words of Jesus, "Without Me you can do nothing." They confess our estrangement from God, the coldness of our devotion, and the weakness of our will apart from God. They look to God and seek God's help in every need.

4. *The prayers focus on the soul's relationship to God.* There is in them a concern for sound teaching and a gratitude for Word and Sacrament. There is a concern for Christian morality and for relationships with other people. But above all, the prayers speak of the individual in our personal relationship with God.

5. *The prayers breathe a spirit of love.* They delight in God's love for us and sing the believer's love for God. A friend of mine said, "When I read a book like this, I realize how little I love God."

My prayer for you is that these prayers, written so long ago, may live for you. May they speak to you and enable you to speak to God, the God who loves you, who has given you life, who has redeemed you from sin and death, and who empowers you daily with God's Spirit. To God be glory and honor to all ages.

RONALD KLUG

11

Help me, Lord Jesus, to rest in you
above all created things,
above all health and beauty,
above all glory and honor,
above all dignity and power,
above all knowledge and thought,
above all wealth and talent,
above all joy and gladness,
above all fame and praise,
above all sweetness and comfort,
above all hope and promise,
above all merit and desire,
above all gifts and favors you may send,
above all angels and archangels and all the hosts of heaven,
above all things visible and invisible,
and above everything
that is not yourself,
O my God.

O my Lord Jesus,
trusting in your great goodness
and mercy,
I come to you
as a sick patient comes to a Healer,
as one who is hungry and thirsty to the Fountain of Life,
as a beggar to the King of heaven,
as a servant to the Lord,
as a creature to the Creator,
and as a desolate person to a kind and compassionate Comforter.
You know me,
that I have no goodness of my own to merit your blessing.
Therefore I confess my unworthiness,
I acknowledge your goodness,
I praise your kindness,
and I give thanks for your boundless love.

All that I am and all that I have
are yours, O Lord.
Yet you serve me
more than I serve you.
The heaven and earth,
the stars and planets,
and all that is in them
obey your laws day by day—
all in our service.
You have even appointed the angels
as our servants.
But above all this,
you yourself stoop to serve us,
and you have promised to give yourself to us.
How then can I repay you for all this goodness?
If only I could serve you faithfully all the days of my life!
If only I could serve you as I wish for even one day!
For you alone are worthy of all honor,
service, and praise
forever.
You are truly my Lord and my God,
and I your poor servant
bound to serve you with all my strength
and to praise you without weariness.
This is my wish and desire,
that I may always glorify and praise you.
Therefore, O Lord, I ask you to supply
whatever is lacking in me,
for it is a great honor and glory to serve you
and to love you above all else.
For those who freely serve you
are richly blessed;

and those who discipline themselves for your sake
receive the comfort of the Holy Spirit;
and those who enter on the narrow way,
find great freedom of spirit.

Lord, you know what is best for me.
Give me what you will
and when you will
and as much as you will.
Do with me as you think best
and as it pleases you
and brings you the most honor.
Place me where you will
and use me according to your wisdom.
I am in your hand
as your servant
ready to do all that you command.
I want to live,
not for myself,
but for you.
I want to serve you
fittingly and perfectly.

Lord, I know that nothing can comfort me,
nor can I rest content in anything created,
but in you alone, O my God,
whom I long to see eternally.
I cannot see you now
while I am in this earthly life,
but I must trust you patiently
and keep you first in my mind.
During the time they lived here
your holy saints,
who now rejoice with you in heaven,
waited the coming of your glory
with great faith and patience.
What they believed,
I believe.
What they hoped to enjoy,
I hope to enjoy.
Where by your grace they have arrived,
I too hope to come.
Until then I walk in faith,
strengthened by their example.
Until then I have the holy scriptures
for my comfort and the mirror of my life,
and I have for my refuge and remedy
your most holy sacrament.
I realize that two things are essential
for me in this world;
without them this life would be unbearable.
I need food and light.
These you have given me:
your blessed sacrament for the refreshment

of my soul and body
and your Word as a lantern for my feet
to show me the way I shall go.
Without these two gifts,
I cannot live well.
For the Word of God is the light of my soul,
and your sacrament is my bread of life.

Lord, all you say is true.
Let it be done to me according to your Word.
May your truth teach me and guard me
and lead me to a blessed end.
May it free me from every wrong desire
and every confused thought.
Then I will walk with you
in freedom of spirit
and in liberty of heart.

My Lord and my King,
how wonderful are the joys
you keep for those who love you!
How much more will you give those
who love and serve you with all their hearts!
You give them the inexpressible joy of contemplation.
You showed your love for me especially
by creating me when I was not,
and when I wandered far from you,
you led me back again to serve you
and taught me to love you.
O Fountain of eternal love,
how can I forget you,
since you have remembered me so lovingly?
When I was lost,
you showed mercy on me
beyond all I could hope or desire.
You sent me your grace and love
above all I deserve.
What shall I give you in return for all this goodness?
It is no great burden to serve you,
whom all creation is bound to serve.
Rather, it should seem wonderful
that you receive into your service someone like me
and count me among your beloved friends.

O Lord, by seeking myself,
I lost you
and myself as well.
Now in seeking you again,
I have found both myself
and you.
Therefore
I will humble myself all the more
and seek you more diligently.
Dear Lord, you give me more than I deserve,
more than I can ask or even hope for.
Your generosity and goodness never cease to bless
even those who are ungrateful
or who have wandered far from you.
Turn us back to you, O Lord,
that we may be thankful, humble, and devoted to you.
For you are our salvation,
our courage,
and our strength.

Most kind Jesus,
grant me your grace.
Let it be always with me
and work in me
and remain with me to the end.
Grant that I may always desire and will
whatever is most pleasing and acceptable to you.
Let your will be mine,
and let my will always follow yours and conform to it.
Grant that I may die to all selfish ambition,
and for your sake be willing to be despised and unknown.
Grant above all else that I may find
in you perfect peace and rest
for my body and soul.
For apart from you
everything is hard and restless.
In the true peace that is in you,
the one highest and eternal good,
I will live and find my rest.

O Lord of love,
you know my many weaknesses and needs,
and how often I am discouraged, tempted,
troubled, and stained by sin.
I come to you for healing,
and I pray for your strength and comfort.
Lord, you know all things,
to you my inward thoughts are open,
and you alone can perfectly guide and help me.
You know what I need,
and you understand all my shortcomings.
Lord, I come to you like a poor beggar,
asking for your help.
Feed me, for I am hungry.
Warm my coldness by the fire of your love.
Illumine my blindness by the light of your presence.
Turn all irritating and frustrating things into patience,
and help me to turn away from everything harmful.
Lift up my heart to you in heaven,
and let me not wander aimlessly on the earth.
You alone are my food and drink,
my love and my joy,
and my highest good.

Prayers from the *Imitation of Christ*

My God and my love,
you are mine, and I am yours.
Deepen your love in me, O Lord,
that I may learn how joyful it is to serve you.
Let your love take hold of me
and raise me above myself,
that I may be filled with devotion
because of your goodness.
Then I will sing to you a song of love.
I will follow you,
and my soul will never grow tired of praising you.
Let me love you more than myself,
and love myself only for your sake.
Let me love all others
in you and for you,
as your law of love commands.

Lord, help me in my troubles,
for human help is unpredictable.
Often I have found no friendship
where I expected it,
and often I have found friendship where I least expected it.
I have decided it is useless
to trust in people,
because certain trust and help is found alone in you, O Lord.
In all that happens to us, we bless you, O Lord our God.
We are weak and unstable and easily deceived.
We cannot guard ourselves so carefully
that we do not fall into doubt or deception.
But whoever trusts in you, O Lord,
and seeks you with a pure heart,
does not easily fall.
And if we encounter any trouble,
no matter how great,
we will soon be delivered by you and comforted,
for you never forsake those who trust in you.
Rare is a faithful friend
who stands by through all troubles.
But you, Lord, are faithful in all things,
and there is none like you.

O Lord, what can I trust in this life?
And what is my greatest comfort on earth?
It is you, O Lord,
whose love is without limit.
When have I ever done well without you?
When have I ever been harmed when you were present?
I would rather be poor with you,
than rich without you.
I would rather be a wanderer on earth with you,
than to be in heaven without you.
For where you are,
there is heaven.
And where you are not,
there is death and hell.
You are everything that I long for;
therefore I will earnestly pray to you.
There is no one who can help me
except you alone, O my God.
For you are my hope,
you are my assurance,
you are my strength,
you are my comfort,
and my most faithful helper
in every need.

O God, living Truth,
make me one with you
in perfect love.
Without you
all that I read or hear or see
wears me out.
In you
is all I will or can desire.
Let all teachers be silent before you;
let the whole creation be quiet,
so that you alone, O Lord,
may speak to me.
The more I am united with you,
the more I can understand,
for from you, O Lord,
I receive light and understanding.

Speak, Lord, for I am listening.
Do not let Moses or the other prophets speak to me,
but rather you yourself,
who inspire and enlighten the prophets.
You alone, without them, can teach me perfectly;
but without you, they can do little for me.
The prophets can speak words,
but they cannot convey the spirit of the words.
They may speak beautifully,
but if you are silent,
they cannot set the heart on fire.
They teach the letter,
but you open the understanding.
They reveal spiritual mysteries,
but you unlock the meaning of the secrets.
They teach us your commandments,
but you help us obey them.
They point the way,
but you give us the strength to walk in it.
They work from the outside,
but you illuminate and instruct the heart.
Therefore speak to me yourself, O living Truth,
so that I do not die without bearing fruit,
being warned from the outside,
but not warmed from within.
For I will be more strictly judged
if I have heard your Word,
but have not obeyed it;
if I have known it,
but not loved it;
if I believe it,
but do not live it.

Therefore, speak to me yourself,
for you have the words of eternal life.
Speak them to me and comfort my soul.
Transform my life to your everlasting praise,
honor, and glory.

What are we to you, O Lord?
Can the clay glorify itself
against the one who shapes it?
Can a person whose heart is subject to God's truth
be deceived by empty words?
The whole world could not lift up to false pride
one who is subject to God.
Nor could those who have fixed their whole hope in God
be moved by flattering tongues.
They know that those who speak empty words are nothing;
they will pass away
as quickly as the sound of their words.
But the truth of the Lord stands forever.

O Lord, my God,
you are all my riches,
and everything I have is from you.
You alone are good, just, and holy.
You can do all things
give all things,
fill all things with your goodness.
Remember your mercies, Lord,
and fill my heart with your grace.
How can I endure the miseries of this life
unless you comfort me with your mercy?
Do not turn your face from me,
do not delay coming to me.
If you withdraw your Spirit from me,
my soul will become like a waterless desert,
thirsty for you.
You, Lord, are all my wisdom and learning.
Before the world was made
and before I was born,
you knew me,
and you know me now as I am.
Teach me, Lord, to do your will
and to live in a worthy and humble way
in your presence.

Lord, I bring before you
the needs of my parents, friends,
brothers, sisters,
all whom I love,
and all who have asked me to pray for them.
I pray that they may experience your help
and the gift of your comfort,
protection from all dangers,
deliverance from all sin,
and freedom from pain.
May they give you joyful thanks and praise.
I also bring before you
all those who have in any way
offended or insulted me,
or done me any harm.
I also remember those
whom I have hurt or offended or troubled
by what I said or did
knowingly or unknowingly.
Lord, in your mercy, forgive all our sins against one another.
Take from our hearts
all suspicion, hard feelings,
anger, dissension,
and whatever else may diminish the love
we should have for one another.
Have mercy, O Lord, on all who ask your mercy.
Give grace to all who need it,
that we may finally come to eternal life.

Lord, I know that you sometimes permit
trouble and temptation to come to me.
I cannot escape them,
but, driven by my need,
I must come to you for help
that you may work this out for my good.
O God, I feel uneasy and depressed
because of this present trouble.
I feel trapped on every side,
yet I know I have come to this hour,
so that I may learn that you alone
can free me from this predicament.
Lord, deliver me,
for what can I do without you,
helpless as I am?
Lord, give me patience in all my troubles.
Help me, and I will not be afraid,
no matter how discouraged I may be.
Let me bear this trouble patiently
until the storm has passed
and my heart is calm again.
Your power, Lord, can take this trouble from me,
as you have done many times before.
No matter how hard it is for me,
it is easy for you, O Lord.

Lord, I have great need of your grace,
if I am to grow spiritually to the stage
where no created thing
can keep me from perfect contemplation of you.
For as long as any transitory thing
enslaves me or holds me back,
I cannot come freely to you.
One who desired to come to you freely said,
"Who will give me wings like the dove,
that I may fly into the bosom of my Savior
and be at rest?"
Who is more at rest
than the one with a single purpose?
And who is more free
than the one who desires nothing but God?

I am left here, O Lord, a poor exile in a hostile land,
where there is constant war and great calamities.
Comfort me in my exile and ease my sorrow,
for my whole desire and longing is for you alone.
Everything the world offers me for comfort
is only another burden.
I long for spiritual growth
but I cannot achieve it.
I want to hold on to spiritual things,
but my daily worries and undisciplined desires
always drag me down.
I want my mind to rise above these concerns,
but my body holds me captive.
Thus I fight within myself;
for my spirit longs for heaven,
but the rest of me holds on to earth.
Do not abandon me, O Lord.
Break the power of the Enemy over me.
Enable me to discipline my mind
and the powers of my soul.
Help me to forget all worldly things
and to reject all temptations to sin.
Help me, everlasting Truth,
so that no worthless things may have power over me.
Come, heavenly sweetness,
and let all bitterness of sin fall from me.

O Lord, your providence
will order my life much better
than all I can do or say for myself.
Whenever I do not put all my trust in you,
I find only insecurity.
Lord, keep my will steadfast and true to you,
for I know that everything you plan for me is good.
If it is your will that I be in the light,
blessed be your name.
If it is your will that I be in darkness,
may you also be blessed.
If you choose to comfort me,
blessed be your name.
And if you wish me to live in trouble and without comfort,
may you be equally blessed.
Lord, I will gladly bear
whatever you allow to happen to me.
From your hand I will gladly accept
good and bad,
sweet and bitter,
joy and sorrow.
In all circumstances
I will thank you.
Only keep me from sin, Lord,
and I will fear neither death nor hell.
As long as you do not reject me
and blot my name from the book of life,
then no trouble that comes
can ever harm me.

Lord, I have called you,
and I have longed for you.
Because you first moved me to seek you,
I am ready to give up everything for you.
May you be blessed, O Lord,
for showing such goodness to me,
according to the richness of your mercy.
What more can I say or do, Lord?
I can only humble myself before you
and remember my own shortcomings.
There is none like you, O Lord,
in heaven or earth.
All your works are good;
your judgments are wise and just;
by your providence you govern the universe.
Eternal praise and glory to you,
O Wisdom of the Father.
Let my body and soul,
my voice and my heart,
and all creation
join to praise and bless you.

Forgive me, Lord,
when in my prayers
I think of other things than you.
I confess that I am often led astray by many distractions,
and my mind wanders.
I think about whatever comes into my head,
and what comes in are the things I care about most.
For whatever is immediately delightful
or has become pleasant by habit
is what comes most readily to mind.
For this reason, you, who are the Truth, have said,
"Where your treasure is,
there will be your heart."
If I love heaven,
I gladly think of heavenly things.
If I love the world,
I think about its pleasures and worry about its problems.
If I love my body,
I think about what is pleasing to it.
If I love my spirit,
I think of that which contributes to my spiritual welfare.
Whatever it is I love,
I am eager to think and speak about.
Blessed are those
who look to you alone,
and have disciplined themselves,
overcoming their uncontrolled thoughts
and desires by the power of the Spirit,
in order to offer prayers
to you with a quiet mind.

O Lord, I have great need of your grace
in fullest measure,
to overcome my natural tendency to sin.
For while I inwardly agree with your commandments
knowing they are good, just, and holy,
and that all sin is evil and to be avoided,
I often yield to sin
when I follow sensuality rather than reason.
While I will to do good,
I do not have the strength to achieve it.
I make many good resolutions,
but because of my own weakness,
I fall back and fail
and can make no progress.
O Lord, how necessary, therefore, is your grace,
if I am to begin well, to continue well, and to end well.
For without you I can do nothing good,
but in you and by the power of your grace,
all things are possible.

O Father, ever to be praised,
the hour has come for me to be tested.
It is right that I should now suffer for your sake.
This is a time, known to you from eternity,
in which I will seem for a while to be utterly overwhelmed.
Yet let me inwardly feel your presence.
I will be ridiculed by people, humiliated,
crushed by weariness and suffering,
but I will rise again in the light of a new dawn
and receive glory in your heavenly kingdom.
O holy Father, you have planned it to be so,
and it is done as you have commanded.
To your friends you give this privilege:
for love of you to suffer and be troubled in the world.
Nothing happens on earth
without your knowledge or permission.
Lord, it is good that I have been humbled,
that I may learn how you think
and banish all conceit and presumption.
It is good for me that I have been humiliated,
that I may learn from it
to seek help and comfort from you
rather than from other people.

O Lord, you are always the same,
and always will be the same —
always good, just, and holy,
always ordering all things
according to your loving wisdom.
But I, always more inclined to evil than to good,
never remain the same,
but change many times a day.
Yet when you touch me with your helping hand,
things are better for me.
For you alone,
with no human aid,
can assist and strengthen me,
so that I will no longer be unstable,
but be wholly settled in you
and there find perfect rest.

Open my heart to understand your laws
and teach me to walk according to your ways.
Help me to know your will
and to remember your many blessings,
so that I may give you proper thanks for them.
I know and confess
that I am not yet able
to give you suitable thanks,
even for the least of your blessings.
When I consider your boundless generosity,
my spirit reels before its greatness.

I thank you, Lord,
that you have not ignored my sin,
but have punished me,
sending me sorrows and troubles
within and without.
Heavenly Physician of the soul,
you wound and heal,
you drag down,
and raise up again,
so that I may learn the littleness of my own power
and may trust more fully in you.
O Lord, your discipline teaches me,
your wounding heals me.
Make me a humble disciple,
that I may walk according to your will.
To you I commit myself and all I am.
You know all things,
and nothing is hidden from you.
You know what is helpful for me,
and how trouble helps to scour away the rust of sin.
Do not reject me because of my sinful life,
which is well known to you,
but do with me as you wish.

O Lord God, just judge,
strong and patient,
who understands our weakness and wickedness,
be my strength and comfort in every need.
My own conscience is inadequate,
but you understand what is unknown to me.
Therefore I should humble myself
whenever I am criticized
and patiently endure it.
Forgive me, Lord,
for the many times I have failed in this,
and give me greater patience
in the future.
I obtain pardon only by believing in your mercy,
not by trusting in my own works
or by defending my own innocence.
Even though I may not be aware of all my faults,
this does not excuse me.
Apart from your mercy,
no one can be justified in your sight.

Others seek their own interest,
but you, Lord, seek only my salvation and welfare,
and you turn all things to my good.
Even if you permit me to be tempted and troubled,
you do this for my benefit.
In times of testing like this,
you are as worthy of my praise
as when you fill me with spiritual comfort.
So in you, Lord, I place my whole trust.
In you I bear patiently all my troubles,
for without you I find only instability and weakness.
Many worldly friends will be no help;
powerful advocates are useless;
wise counselors have no sound advice;
learned books give no comfort;
and no secret place can protect me,
if you, Lord, are not by my side
to help, comfort, counsel, instruct, and defend.
All things that seem to bring happiness and peace
are worthless without you,
for they cannot give true and lasting happiness.
You alone are the source of all good things,
the fullness of life,
the depth of wisdom,
and our greatest comfort in every need.

O Lord, set me on fire with your presence,
and turn me to yourself
that I may be wholly dedicated to you.
Let me be united in spirit with you,
by the grace of inward union
and by the melting of burning love.
Do not send me away
hungry or thirsty,
but treat me mercifully
as you have dealt with your servants in times past.
How wonderful it would be
if I were wholly on fire for you
and dead to self!
For you, Lord, are the fire unquenchable,
burning forever.
You are the love that purifies the heart
and enlightens the mind.

O Lord, a truly devout person
begrudges all the attention spent on
food and drink and clothing and other bodily needs.
Help me to use these things with moderation,
and not be overly concerned about them.
It is not right or possible to ignore them,
for we must take care of our bodies.
But your holy law forbids us
from craving luxuries
or things that prop up our self-importance.
I ask you, then, O Lord,
to govern and guide me
that I may learn to live simply at all times.

O Lord, my God,
you are above all things.
You alone are most good,
most powerful, most sufficient,
most complete,
most sweet and comforting.
You alone are most beautiful,
most able, and most glorious above all things.
In you all goodness is gathered together,
fully and perfectly,
now and forever.
Therefore, whatever you give me,
besides yourself, O Lord,
is small and unsatisfying to me.
For my heart cannot rest or find perfect peace,
until it rises above all your gifts
to rest in you alone.

Lord, make possible for me by grace
what is impossible to me by nature.
You know how little I can bear to suffer,
how quickly I am discouraged
by a little trouble.
I pray that I may accept and even love
all the troubles that you permit to come to me.
To suffer for you and be troubled for you
is good and profitable for my soul.

Lord, I confess my sinfulness
and acknowledge my weakness.
Often it is only a little thing
that defeats me
and makes me slow to do what is right.
I resolve to act bravely,
but a little temptation comes,
and I find myself in great anxiety.
And when I feel most secure,
I am almost overcome by the smallest temptation.
Consider my weakness, O Lord,
for you know it better than anyone else.
Even when I do not yield to these temptations,
they trouble and disturb me,
and I grow weary of living constantly in conflict.
So I come to you for help, O Lord.
Strengthen me with spiritual strength,
so that the old enemy, the devil,
whom I must fight endlessly,
may have no power over me.
Strengthen me so that my flesh,
still not subject to the Spirit,
may not gain the upper hand.

Blessed may you be, heavenly Father,
father of my Lord Jesus Christ,
for you remember me, your poor servant,
and you comfort me with your presence,
even though I am not worthy of it.
When you come into my heart, everything in me rejoices.
You are my glory,
the joy of my heart,
my hope and my refuge in time of trouble.
Because my love for you is still weak
and my virtue imperfect,
I need your strength and comfort.
Come to me often, therefore,
and teach me the way of holiness.
Free me from all evil and confusion
that I may be able to love you,
strong to suffer for you,
and firm to persevere in you.

Most loving God,
keep me from being overwhelmed
by the cares and busyness of this life.
Keep me, too, from being overly concerned
with the needs of my body
and from being enslaved by the pursuit of pleasure.
Save me, too, from the dangers to my spirit,
so that I am not crushed or overwhelmed
by depression or anxiety.
I do not ask to be delivered only from the emptiness
that many pursue so desperately,
but also from the miseries that weigh me down
and keep me from experiencing your presence
freely, as often as I would like.
O Lord God, my joy above all joys,
turn to bitterness
all pleasures that draw me away from eternal joys.
Do not let flesh and blood overcome me,
nor the world with its values deceive me,
nor the devil with all his cunning ensnare me.
Give me strength to resist,
patience to endure,
and constancy to persevere.
In place of all the pleasures of the world,
give me the rich comfort of your Holy Spirit,
and in place of self-centeredness
fill me with love of your holy name.

Prayers from the *Imitation of Christ*

O Lord, all that we have,
in body or soul,
without or within,
natural or supernatural,
are your gifts
and reveal you
as a loving and good God.
Whether we receive more or less,
all are your gifts,
and without you we would have nothing.

Whoever has received more
may not boast
as though they had received more because of their own merits,
or despise those who have received less.
The people who are greatest and most pleasing to you
are those who claim the least for themselves
and who humbly and devoutly
return thanks to you for those gifts.
Those who view themselves humbly
are more fit to receive from you greater things.

Whoever has received less
should not be sad or envious.
Rather they should lift their minds to you
and praise your goodness,
because your gifts are given
freely, generously, and lovingly,
without respect of persons.
You alone know what is best
for each person to receive.
All good things come from you,
and in all things you are to be praised.

My Lord Jesus, do not be far from me,
but come quickly and help me
for evil thoughts have risen in my mind,
and I am terrified by fears of the future.
How shall I break their power over me?
How shall I go unhurt without your help?
O Lord,
you have promised,
"I myself will prepare your way,
leveling mountains and hills.
I will open the gates of the prison,
and reveal to you
the hidden treasures of spiritual knowledge."
O Lord, do as you have said,
and let your coming
drive away all evil thoughts.
This is my hope and my only comfort —
to turn to you in every trouble,
to put all my trust in you,
to call inwardly upon you,
and to wait for your comfort with patience.

My God and my All!
When you are present,
everything is pleasant and joyful.
When you are absent,
all things are irritating and unsatisfying.
When you come,
you bring rest to my heart,
true peace, and new joy,
for nothing can give us lasting joy without you.
Whoever knows your joy
will find joy in all things.
But whoever finds no joy in you,
will find no joy in anything.
Those who love the world apart from you
fail to find wisdom,
and selfish pleasures lead only to emptiness.
Those who follow you
by leading a moderate and self-disciplined life
are truly wise.
They are led from illusion to truth
and from flesh to spirit.
They find delight in God,
and whatever good they find in created things,
they attribute to the glory and praise of God the Creator.
For they understand how great is the difference
between the creature and the Creator,
between the passing and the eternal,
between created light and Light uncreated.

O Lord, I long for the joy of inward peace,
the peace of your chosen children,
who are strengthened and refreshed by you.
Without your help
I cannot find this peace.
When you withdraw yourself from me,
as you sometimes have done,
I cannot follow the way of your commandments.
Instead I feel crushed
because I no longer experience your strength
which protects me from all temptations and dangers.
But if you come to me again
and fill my heart with peace and joy,
then my spirit will be full of song
and entirely devoted to your praise.

O God, heavenly Father,
blessed be your name now and forever.
As you will things to be,
they are,
and what you do
is always good.
Let me, your servant,
find joy in you
and not in myself
or in any other thing.
You alone, O Lord, are my joy,
my hope, and my crown,
my gladness, and my honor,
I have nothing that is not your gift,
and I have no merit of my own.
All things that you have created
and that you have given
are yours, O Lord.

O blessed Lord,
you make the poor in spirit rich in virtues,
and you make the rich humble in heart.
Come, descend on me.
Fill me with your comfort
so that my soul does not faint
because of weariness and dryness.
I pray, Lord, that I may find grace in your sight,
for your grace is sufficient for me,
even though I lack the things my nature desires.
Though I am troubled and tempted on every side,
I will fear no evil
as long as your grace is with me.
Your grace is my strength, my comfort,
my counsel, and my help.
It is stronger than my enemies
and wiser than all the wise.
Your grace is the teacher of truth,
and the light of the heart,
and comfort in trouble.
It banishes sorrow,
drives away fear,
nourishes devotion,
and produces repentance.
Without grace, I am only a dry stick to be thrown away.
Therefore, O Lord, let your grace always go before me
and follow me, through your son Jesus Christ.
Amen.

Prayers from the *Imitation of Christ*

Strengthen me, O God,
by the power of your Holy Spirit.
Remove from me all useless anxiety
and give me inner courage.
Let me never be enticed away from you
by the desire for anything else,
but help me to realize
that all things are transitory—
as I am.
In this world nothing is lasting,
and everything is uncertain
and troubling to the spirit.
How wise is the one who understands this!
Give me true spiritual wisdom, Lord,
that I may learn to seek you,
and find you,
and above all to love you.
Enable me to understand all things as they really are.
May I wisely avoid all those who would flatter me
and deal patiently with those who irritate me.
True wisdom cannot be swayed by every wind of words,
and it disregards all deceitful flattery.
If I live by this wisdom,
I will move forward on the road I must travel.

Lord Jesus, you were patient
in your life on earth,
fulfilling the will of your Father.
In the same way,
I want to bear myself patiently,
accepting your will
in all things.
I will bear the burdens of this life
as long as it is your will.
Even though this life is hard,
your grace makes it worthwhile.
By your example and the examples of the saints,
this life is made more bearable
and we are saved by your blessed passion
and the atonement of your holy death.

Prayers from the *Imitation of Christ*

O Jesus, brightness of eternal glory,
joy and comfort of all Christian people,
who walk like pilgrims
in this world,
hear the silent cry of my heart:
"How long will my Lord delay in coming?"
Come to me, poor and little as I am,
and bring me joy.
Stretch out your hand
and deliver me from all anguish and pain.
Come, Lord, come,
for without you, my soul is barren and empty.
Come, Lord, come,
for without you, no day or hour is happy.
Without you, my table is without its guest,
for you alone are my joy.
I am like a prisoner in chains
until through the light of your presence,
you visit me to refresh me,
to liberate my spirit,
and to show me your face as my friend.
Let others seek what they will;
there is nothing I will seek,
nothing that can give me joy,
but you alone, my God,
my hope and my everlasting salvation.
I will not keep silent
or cease to pray
until you return to me,
and say to my soul,
"I am here."

Lord Jesus, send the clarity of your light
into my mind
and expel all darkness from my heart.
Fight strongly for me
and drive away the temptations
that rage like wild beasts within me.
Then my conscience will be at peace,
and the praise of your name
will sound within the temple of my soul.
Command the winds and storms of pride to be still,
and the sea of covetousness to be at rest.
Subdue the north wind of the devil's temptation.
Then there will be a great calm within me.

Prayers from the *Imitation of Christ*

Lord Jesus,
be with me
in every place and every time.
May I be willing to give up all human comfort
for the sake of your comfort.
And when I do not experience your comfort
may I find consolation
by submitting to your will
and accepting your testing.
For you will not always be angry,
nor will you condemn me forever.

Oh, what thanks we owe you
because you have showed us the true and holy way
to your eternal kingdom.
Your life is our way,
and by patience we will journey to you,
our Leader and our Home.
If you, Lord, had not gone ahead of us
to show us the way,
who could follow?
How many would have lagged far behind,
if they had not had your example as a guide?
Even now, after we have heard your teachings
and seen your miracles,
we are cold and dull.
What would we have done without them?
Surely we would have fixed our hearts and minds
only on the things of this world.
But now, O Lord, from this blindness
may your great goodness
preserve us.

False pride is a dangerous sickness, O Lord,
because it draws us away from the true glory
we should have in you,
and robs us of heavenly grace.
When people are self-satisfied,
they displease you.
And when they seek popularity,
they lose their integrity.
For true lasting joy is found not in self-glorification,
but in giving glory to you,
not in one's own strength,
but in your name.
Therefore, may your name, and not mine, be praised,
your works, and not mine, glorified.
You alone are my glory.
You alone are the joy of my heart.
I will offer you praise and glory every hour of the day,
but for myself, I will glory only in my weakness.
I will seek the approval that only God can give.
For all human glory,
all this world's honor,
all pride of position,
compared to your glory,
are foolish and empty.
O blessed Trinity,
my God, my truth, my mercy,
to you be all praise, honor,
power, and glory,
through endless ages.

O Lord, there can be no goodness in us
if you withdraw yourself.
No wisdom can benefit us,
if you cease to guide us.
No strength can preserve us,
if you no longer defend.
No purity can be secure,
if you do not guard it.
No watchfulness of our own can protect us,
if you do not keep watch.
If you abandon us,
we are soon lost and perish.
But if you come to us with your grace,
we are lifted up to live again.
We are weak,
but you make us strong.
We are cold and dull,
but by you we are set ablaze.

Help me, Lord, to know all I need to know
and to love all I should love,
to value what most pleases you
and to reject what you consider evil.
Let me not judge superficially according to what I see
nor be influenced by the opinions of the foolish,
but give me true judgment to discern
between things seen and unseen
and always to seek your good will and what pleases you.
Human judgment is often faulty,
and people are often deceived by loving only material things.
Is anyone better just because others think highly of him?
One foolish person only
deceives another.
The higher the flattery,
the greater the humiliation that follows.
No matter what his reputation before other people,
a person is worth only what he is in your eyes —
that much and no more.

O Lord Jesus Christ,
lover of the soul,
Lord of creation,
who will give me wings of true freedom
that I may fly to you,
and be at rest?
When shall I be set free
and taste your sweetness, O Lord?
When shall I become so centered in you
that for love of you I may no longer
be conscious of myself,
but of you alone?
Now I often mourn and complain
about the miseries of life,
because many evil things happen daily
that disturb me and darken my path.
They get in the way and distract me
so I cannot approach you freely
and enjoy your gracious presence.
Therefore I pray
that both my sadness and my desire
may move you to hear me, O Lord.

Prayers from the *Imitation of Christ*

O everlasting Light,
surpassing all created light,
send the beams of your brightness from above,
to purify, gladden, and enlighten me.
Bring life to my spirit
that it may hold to you with boundless joy.
Oh, when will that blessed hour come,
when you will fill me with your presence
and be to me all in all?
Until that gift is given
my joy will be incomplete.
For my old nature is still strong within me;
it is not yet wholly crucified or entirely dead.
The flesh still fights against the spirit,
stirs up conflicts within me,
and does not allow me to live in peace.
But you, O Christ, rule over the power of the sea.
You can calm its raging waves.
Come and help me!
Break the power of the Enemy,
who stirs up this battle within me.
Show the strength of your goodness,
for I have no hope or refuge but in you,
my Lord and my God.

My soul is like the primeval earth —
formless and empty and dark.
Send out the light of your truth, O Lord.
Pour out your grace
on my heart, dry and barren,
and water it with the dew of inward devotion.
Then my soul will bring forth good fruit,
agreeable and pleasing to you.
Lift up my mind
that is now weighed down by sin.
Raise my desire to the love of spiritual things,
so that having tasted heavenly joy,
I may turn from all the passing pleasures of the world.
Free me from all dependence on the temporary satisfaction
that comes from things which soon pass away,
for these can never fully satisfy my longings.
Unite me to you
by the unbreakable bonds of love,
for you alone can satisfy the one who loves you.
Without you, everything else
is empty and worthless.

Prayers from the *Imitation of Christ*

O Lord, how good and peaceful it is
to remain silent about others,
neither believing everything that is said,
nor repeating everything we see and hear.
We should not be blown about by every puff of words.
We should not confide only in a few people,
but always seek you,
who understands us perfectly.
You desire that our whole lives,
inwardly and outwardly,
be ordered according to your will.
A sure way of retaining spiritual grace
is to avoid people and things that lead us astray,
and to seek wholeheartedly
the things that increase our devotion
and better our lives.

Lord, blessed is your holy Word,
sweeter to my mouth than the honeycomb.
What would I do
in all my troubles and trials,
if you did not comfort and strengthen me
with your holy and health-giving Word?
Therefore it does not matter
how many storms or troubled waters
I go through for your sake,
so long as I come at last
to a safe harbor.
Give me a good end
and a joyful passage from this life.
Remember me,
my Lord and my God,
and lead me by a straight path
to your kingdom.
Amen.

Prayers from the *Imitation of Christ*

O Lord, if I come to you
thinking myself better than I am,
my own sins witness against me.
But if I come humbly and honestly,
and see myself as I really am,
then your grace will come to me
and your light will brighten my heart
and give me true understanding of myself,
so that my self-importance will be drowned
in the valley of humbleness.
You show me my true self,
what I have been
and what I have become.
For I am nothing,
and did not know it.
Left to myself,
I will continue to be nothing
but if you help me only a little,
I will be strong again and filled with new joy.
I am amazed at how quickly you can pick me up
after I have fallen.
It is your love, Lord,
that does this,
your love that guides me,
helps me in all my needs,
guards me from many dangers,
and keeps me from unnumbered evils.

Lord, I am not worthy of your comfort
or your company.
You would be just
if you left me needy and desolate.
But you, Lord, are kind and merciful,
and do not wish me to perish,
and so you comfort me
though I do not deserve it.
Although it is painful for me,
I will honestly confess my weaknesses and admit my defects
so that I may obtain your mercy and forgiveness.
In my guilt and confusion,
what can I say?
Only this: "I have sinned, Lord, I have sinned.
Be merciful and forgive."
In true penitence and humility
the hope of pardon is found,
the troubled conscience is cleared,
and lost grace is restored.
We are spared God's anger,
and God and the penitent sinner
meet in the holy embrace of love.

O blessed mansion of the heavenly city!
O bright day of eternity,
which night can never darken,
always illumined by the light of God!
O day of eternal joy and everlasting security!
I long for the dawning of this day
and the end of this present order.
That blessed day in all its glory
already shines on the saints in heaven,
but to those of us who are still pilgrims on earth,
it seems dim and distant.
The citizens of heaven already enjoy that day,
but we exiles on earth,
poor banished children of Eve,
experience bitterness and heaviness
because our days are short and troubled,
filled with sorrow and pain.
Here we are defiled by sin,
ensnared by passions,
tormented by anxiety and fears,
oppressed by cares,
distracted by trivialities,
troubled by temptations,
addicted to pleasure.
O Lord, when will all these miseries come to an end?
When will I be freed from the bondage of sin?
When will my mind be fixed on you alone?
When will I rejoice fully in you?
When will I be truly free,
with no inner confusion
and conflict?

When will I have true peace,
untroubled and secure,
inside and out?
O Lord Jesus, when will I see you face to face?
When shall I have a full vision of your glory?
When will you be all in all to me?
When will I be with you in your kingdom
which you have prepared from eternity
for those you love?

Prayers from the *Imitation of Christ*

I come to you, O Lord,
that I may be blessed by your gift,
rejoicing in the feast
you have prepared for me.
In you I find all that I may or should desire,
for you are my Savior and my Redeemer.
You are my hope, my strength,
my honor and glory.
Let me find joy in you today, Lord,
for I lift up my soul to you.
I wish to receive you with reverence and devotion:
I want to invite you into my house,
as Zacchaeus did,
so that I too may receive your blessing
and be counted among your chosen ones.
My soul desires to receive your body and blood.
My heart longs to be united with you.
Give me yourself,
and it is enough;
nothing but you can satisfy me.
Without you I cannot live.
Therefore I must come to you often
and receive you for my spiritual health.
For deprived of this heavenly food,
I would fall by the wayside.
Because I so quickly grow lukewarm and sluggish,
it is essential for me
to be cleansed and renewed by prayer and confession
and by receiving of your holy sacrament.
O Lord God, Creator and Giver of Life,
how wonderful is your kindness and mercy to me
that you should stoop to visit so poor a creature as I

to refresh me, to satisfy my hunger
with your whole divinity and humanity.
Happy is one who devoutly receives you
with all spiritual joy.
How great a Lord this soul receives!
How beloved a Guest she welcomes into her house!
How delightful a Companion she receives!
How faithful a Friend she accepts,
who receives you!
For you alone are to be loved and desired
before and above all others.

To you, Father of mercy, I lift up my eyes.
In you alone, my God, I put my trust.
Bless and hallow my soul
that it may be your heavenly dwelling.
Let nothing remain in my heart that will offend you.
Have mercy on me and hear the prayer of your servant,
an exile in the country of the shadow of death.
Guard and keep me among the many dangers
of this corruptible life.
Through your grace guide me
in the ways of peace
until I reach my home
of everlasting light.

Prayers from the *Imitation of Christ*

Lord Jesus, your way of life was narrow
and scorned by the world.
Help me to imitate you in bearing whatever burdens
you choose to send.
The servant is not greater than the master,
nor the student greater than the teacher.
Therefore, let me learn from your life
for there I will find holiness and salvation.
Whatever I read or hear other than this
neither refreshes nor delights me.

Lord, I am not worthy of your comfort
nor of any spiritual experience.
When you leave me needy and desolate,
you are treating me as I deserve.
Even though I shed an ocean of tears,
I would not deserve your consolation.
I have earned only suffering and punishment
because I have so often offended you
and done what was evil in your sight.
Yet you are kind and merciful,
and do not want any of your sons and daughters
to be lost.
To demonstrate your love and goodness,
you reach down to bless me
far more than I deserve,
more than I can imagine.

Those who realize their own poverty and shortcomings
need not be depressed or disappointed
but should take comfort in the fact that you, O God,
have chosen the poor, the humble, the despised of the world
to be your friends and servants.
Therefore nothing should give comfort and joy
to those who love you
as much as knowing that your will and purposes
are accomplished in them.
They are more content to be considered small
than others are to be great.
They find as much peace and contentment in last place
as in first.
They are as cheerful at being ignored and rejected
as others who are full of fame and honor.
Your will and honor, O God, are more important
than anything else.
And they will bring us greater comfort and pleasure
than any other blessing that could be given.

O Lord, what will become of us?
We are so upset over a trivial loss.
We work so hard for a little money,
but take so little interest in caring for our souls.
We pay so much attention to unimportant things
and practically forget what is really necessary.
We easily get lost in mundane concerns.
Help us recover our senses and return to you.

Prayers from the *Imitation of Christ*

Lord, grant that I may find you
and give my whole heart to you.
Let no one deceive me or distract me,
but speak to me
as a lover speaks to a beloved,
as friend to friend.
This is what I pray for—
that I may be united completely with you
and that you may fill my whole being.
O Lord, when will I be wholly at one with you,
wholly absorbed in you
and unmindful of myself?
Be in me,
and may I be in you,
so we may remain together forever.
You are indeed my beloved,
preferred over all others.
My spirit wants to abide in you
all the days of my life.
You are the giver of true peace and rest.
Apart from you there is only weariness and sorrow.

Lord Jesus, you have said,
"Come to me all who labor and are heavy laden,
and I will give you rest."
These are your words,
and because they are your words,
I accept them with gratitude and trust.
I receive them gladly so they may be imprinted
deeply on my heart.
Your invitation, so full of pity and love, gives me courage,
while my sins frighten me and weigh me down.
Lord, you say, "Come to me."
You invite me to approach you in faith
if I wish to share in your life.
You invite me, poor and needy,
to the Holy Communion of your body and blood.
But who am I that I should presume to come to you?
How can I, unaware of doing any good,
dare to come?
How can I, who have offended you so often,
invite you into my house?
Yet you say, "Come to me."
Except that you said it, Lord,
who could believe it?
Except that you commanded it,
who would dare approach?

You, Lord, are the holy of holies,
I am the lowest of sinners.
Because I am not worthy to look up to you,
you bend down to me.
You want to be with me
and you invite me to your feast.
You want to give me this heavenly food,
the bread of angels,
yourself,
the living bread come down from heaven
to give life to the world.
You are the source of all love and goodness,
and you are worthy of all my thanks and praise.

O God, unseen Creator of the world,
how wonderfully you treat us.
How lovingly and graciously you care for those
you have chosen as your own,
those to whom you give yourself in Holy Communion.
This gift surpasses all understanding,
and enkindles love in the hearts of your devoted people,
and draws them to you.
True, faithful people who strive to amend their lives
receive in this sacrament strength
and the love of doing what is right.
The wonderful grace of this sacrament is hidden
from unbelievers and those who remain in sin,
but known by God's faithful people.
In this sacrament, grace is given,
strength is restored,
the beauty that was destroyed by sin returns.
We receive the sacrament not only for the healing of our souls,
but also for our bodies.
We are sorry for the lukewarmness and spiritual stagnation
that hinders us from receiving Christ with greater love,
because in him rests all our merit and our hope of salvation.
He is our redemption and sanctification.
He is the comfort of the pilgrims in this world
and the saints in heaven.

Lord, when I consider your greatness
and my smallness,
I am shaken and confused.
If I do not receive you in Holy Communion,
I run from life.
If I receive you unworthily,
I come under your judgment.
What, then, should I do,
my God, my helper, my adviser in every need?
Teach me the right way to prepare myself
for Holy Communion
that I might receive your sacrament
for my well-being
and properly celebrate this holy meal.

O Lord Jesus, how great is the joy of the devout soul
who feasts at your heavenly banquet,
where the food is your very self,
the greatest desire of our hearts.
I long to pour out my tears before you
as Mary Magdalene washed your feet with her tears.
In your presence my heart ought to weep for joy,
because here in your sacrament you are truly present with me,
though hidden under the form of bread and wine.
I could not gaze on you in your naked majesty and glory,
so you accommodate yourself to my weakness
by hiding yourself in this holy sacrament.
I worship the same God whom the angels adore in heaven,
only I live by faith
and they by open sight.
Now I must be content with the light of faith
and walk in it until the day of everlasting light dawns
and all shadows pass away.
When that which is perfect has come,
there will be no need of sacraments,
for we shall enjoy God's presence,
seeing God face to face, forever,
transformed from glory to glory
by God's own nature.

Prayers from the *Imitation of Christ*

O Lord, I long to receive you
with reverence and holy love,
as many saints and devout believers
longed to receive you in Holy Communion.
Though I fall far short of their devotion,
I offer whatever love is in my heart.
I want to hold nothing back,
but offer myself and all I have.
O my God, my Creator and Redeemer,
accept the praises and blessing
I rightly owe you because of your goodness.
These I offer you, now and every day, every moment.
I ask the angels and all God's faithful people
to join in my thanks and praise.
Let all peoples, nations, and languages
praise and exalt your holy name
with great joy and deep devotion.
May all who reverently and devoutly celebrate this sacrament
receive it in faith
and find grace and mercy
at your holy table.

It is a wonderful thing to ponder and believe,
transcending all our understanding,
that you, Lord, true God and true man,
are fully present in the bread and wine.
You are Lord of all things,
in need of nothing,
yet you live in us by means of this sacrament.
Keep my spirit and body clean
so that with a glad and clear conscience
I may celebrate your holy sacrament
and receive it for my eternal salvation.
Rejoice, my soul, and thank God for this great gift,
for this unique comfort, given us in this valley of tears.
As often as we celebrate this mystery
and receive the body and blood of Christ,
we receive salvation and share in all the merits of Christ.
Therefore we should prepare ourselves
with an alert mind to ponder this mystery of salvation.
Each time we receive this Holy Communion
it should be as new as if it were the day
that Christ entered the womb of the Virgin
to become our brother,
or when he suffered on the cross
for our salvation.

Prayers from the *Imitation of Christ*

O Lord Jesus, I ask you graciously and kindly
to supply whatever is lacking in me.
I work and sweat.
My soul is twisted with sorrow.
I am unsettled by temptations,
oppressed by weaknesses.
No one can free me or save me
except you, Lord God.
To you I entrust myself and all I have,
so that you may guard and guide me to eternal life.
Receive me for the praise and glory of your name,
you who have given your body and blood
to be my food and drink.
O Lord God, grant that by receiving your holy sacrament,
I may grow in love and devotion to you.
Through this sacrament you comfort us in our troubles,
raise us from despair to hope.
You refresh and enlighten us
so that we who were sluggish and cold
are refreshed and empowered by this holy food and drink.
All this you do from your great love for your people.
That they may truly know from experience
their own weakness
and the goodness they receive from you.
By ourselves we are cold, dull, and apathetic,
but through you we become warm, alive, and devout.
Who can drink from the fountain of goodness
and not carry goodness with them?
Who can stand by the fire and not be warmed?
You, Lord, are the Fountain always overflowing
and the fire ever burning.

Now that we have begun the journey,
we dare not go backward or give up.
Let us move forward together.
Jesus will be with us.
For Jesus' sake we have taken up the cross.
For Jesus let us persevere.
He will be our guide,
our leader,
our helper.
He has already scouted out the road.
Let us follow courageously,
ready to die bravely in the struggle,
never turning away from the cross.

Prayers from the *Imitation of Christ*

O Lord God, give me your blessing
so I may reverently and devoutly approach your sacrament.
Rouse me from spiritual sleep and free me from apathy.
Come to me with your salvation,
that my soul may experience the love
hidden in Holy Communion.
Open my eyes to see the mystery
and strengthen me to believe it with unshakable faith.
This is your work, not a human action.
This is your creation, not our invention.
By ourselves we cannot understand these mysteries,
which are beyond the knowledge of angels.
How then can I, an unworthy sinner,
take hold of such a mystery,
except by faith, with simplicity of heart,
in response to your invitation?
I firmly believe that you are present in this sacrament
as God and man.
It is your will that I receive you
and be united with you in love.
Therefore, I ask your mercy and pray for your grace
that I may be united in your love
and seek nothing but you.
This high and holy sacrament
is for the healing of soul and body
and the cure for every spiritual sickness.

By this sacrament our weaknesses are cured,
our passions restrained,
our temptations overcome.
By it we receive grace,
virtue is strengthened,
faith is made strong,
hope is renewed,
love is kindled into flame.

INDEX OF FIRST LINES

Prayers from the *Imitation of Christ*

BIBLIOGRAPHY

There are many good translations of the *Imitation of Christ*. A traditional one is by Harold C. Gardiner, based on the English version by Richard Whitford around 1530 (New York: Doubleday Image Books, 1955). A more contemporary translation is by William C. Creasey (Macon, Georgia: Mercer University Press, 1989).

For background reading, you may wish to consult the following books:

Bernhard Christensen, *The Inward Pilgrimage: An Introduction to Christian Spiritual Classics* (Minneapolis: Augsburg, 1996).

Bradley P. Holt, *Thirsty for God: A Brief History of Christian Spirituality,* (Minneapolis: Augsburg, 1993).

Other Books in the Classic Prayer Series:

William Barclay, *Prayers for Help and Healing*
A chapter on Christianity and healing followed by more than 100 prayers for help and healing, including morning and evening prayers for hospital stays, prayers for festivals and special days, and for those engaged in healing.

Herbert F. Brokering, editor. *Luther's Prayers*
Prayers based on the Ten Commandments, the Apostles' Creed, and the Lord's Prayer, as well as for many occasions in the Christian life.

George MacDonald, *Diary of an Old Soul*
A prayer for each day of the year, reflecting on some aspect of God's relationship to us.